CW00919851

The Life & Times
of a 'Tankie' from
Lincolnshire
in the Great War
including a short history of the Tank

John C Allen

First published by Barny Books
All rights reserved

ISBN No: 978.1.906542.96.2

Publishers: Barny Books
                www.barnybooks.co.uk

This 'personnel publication' has been researched from printed works, war diaries, family records, photographs and artefacts.

Acknowledgements and References are given at the end of the text.

This is part of the Once Upon A Wartime Series No: 24

Cover design: Sam Jackson (sjacko911@gmail.com)
Designed from an illustration provided by the author

Contents

Preface

The inspiration for researching and collating the following information on the short life of my Great Uncle, Cyril Sheldon Allen, known as Sid, was the passing on of his medals and other artefacts from the Great War of 1914 – 1918, by my late father also named Cyril (known as Syd) in 2009.

When volunteering with his brothers Henry and Bertram into the British Army he no doubt like many others, thought he was engaging in a war of short duration in continental Europe.

Having been employed in the Mechanical Engineering Department of John Lysaght's Ltd recently commissioned iron and steel-works (the first integrated iron and steel plant in the country), and being the proud owner of a 'belt driven' Norton Brooklands Road Special motorcycle, Cyril was no doubt selected by the Army recruiting staff for his motorcycle and mechanical skills and experiences and was transferred to the Motor Machine Gun Service.

The first stages of the war were fought on traditional methods - the infantry making fixed bayonet charges into the enemy lines, followed by the cavalry with their lances. The introduction of the machine gun made a change in fighting tactics where it was possible to 'cut down' rows of approaching attackers in one broad sweep of the weapon.

Development of the 'Landships' as they were known was at the agricultural engineering works of William Fosters in Lincoln. (They were labelled as water carrying tanks for security purposes.) Cyril was transferred to the Heavy Branch MGC, later to become the Tank Corps. This was given the task of crewing the new armoured mechanical fighting machine, now known as the Tank.

At this point in the war, the fighting on both sides had been carried out by infantry supported by artillery and cavalry, armed with howitzers, machine guns and rifles. An interesting statistic is that from mobilisation to the 11th November 1918, the Army Remount Service had provided over 896,000 horses and mules to the Western Front as compared to 121,000 motorised vehicles.

With the introduction of the Tank there was no preconceived ideas on how the machine would be engaged at the battlefront and the training centre had pre-occupational difficulties. Under the haste and pressure of the times, this was no easy task. The entire system had to be thought through from the beginning and continually modified by the experiences of early engagement on the battlefield. In early 1917 the Tank was still a comparatively untested fighting machine, with many faults and weaknesses developing on the Mark I, the first model of the Tank. Not until the Mark IV machine was introduced could a guarantee as to its mechanical reliability be given.

The invention of the Tank grabbed the attention of the media of the day and onward to the public. Another technology, one which we readily accept today, was the development of wireless systems for reporting from the front lines, keeping pace with the attack back to headquarters with the Tanks 'on the move'. Not 'solid state, transistors or glass cased thermionic valves', but spark induction coils, as seen from the recent inventions of Marconi, primarily used by the maritime industry. By all accounts, the British Expeditionary Force (BEF) on crossing into mainland Europe through Belgium and France into the headlong advance of the German Army, had a total of four wireless telegraphy transmitters (senders) and receivers (tuners), one based at headquarters and three deployed by the cavalry.

The Tank, as a new fighting weapon, had been threatened with many crises and many of the 'Top Brass' foresaw them as a gimmick on the battle field. This point was no better endorsed than what happened in the Third Battle of Ypres. The ground on which the Tanks were required to perform was practically all reclaimed swamp land, including Ypres and St Omer which a few hundred years before, were both seaports. After prolonged rainfall and the shelling of drainage dykes, how did one move a weight of twenty eight tons of metal through a morass of mud and water? This resulted in most of the units becoming bogged down, with the battle-ground becoming known as the 'Tank graveyard'.

It was at Ypres that Cyril of No 11 Section, No 3 Company, had volunteered in assisting the Commanding Officer from another Section (Section 12) to lay out tapes over the route for the officers four Tanks to follow into battle. This took over three days and nights under heavy enemy gun-fire. It was this action and the consequences following it, which saw him awarded the Distinguished Conduct Medal for, "grit and determination under heavy fire," as cited by Major General Hugh Elles on a signed certificate sent to Cyril.

It wasn't until the Battle of Cambrai, with an uncultivated open chalk rolling plateau, that the Tank was to prove its worth on this hardened ground material. The British and her allies were to score a surprise tactical victory which broke the mould of trench warfare and pointed to the future. On the first day, 'Aggressive II', the Tank in which Cyril was a crew member, was the unit to fight its way nearest to the township of Cambrai, before becoming 'knocked out' by an enemy shell.

Sadly, this is where Cyril was killed, as described later in the text, which I hope conveys the conditions that the 'Tankies' experienced.

Since many informative literary works have been written on the various battles, equipment, armaments and strategies employed, I have based my work more on the individual experiences that Cyril would have sustained within his service to both the Machine Gun and Tank Corps.

Every year, nine days after Remembrance Day on the 20th of November, the men of the Royal Tank Regiment with its origins in the Tank Corps, celebrate "Cambrai Day" wherever they may be which, sadly, was the date Gunner C S Allen DCM was killed in action.

John Cyril Allen

Private Cyril Sheldon Allen, DCM, Tank Corps

08 November 1892 – 20 November 1917

The Life and Times of Gunner C S Allen. DCM

Chapter 1   Early Life

The short life of Cyril Sheldon Allen began with his birth on the 8th of November 1892 at the estate village of Normanby Hall in North Lincolnshire. He was the third surviving son of Mr and Mrs Ernest Sheldon Allen who originally resided at Ivy Cottage within the village. Ernest was the head gardener to Sir Berkeley Sheffield of Normanby Hall, as recorded in The Hull Times of 25th October 1913. He had at that date been at Normanby Hall and Park for thirty seven years, and for most of those years in that position. The gardens covered eight acres with five miles of walks within the grounds. Overall the Park covered three hundred acres and contained in excess of two hundred head of deer.

The Sheffield family were the major land and property owners in the villages close to the Hall. All the dwellings in the village of Normanby were leased to workers on the estate. Some dwellings were 'nominated' for the holders of certain jobs. As head gardener, Cyril's father resided in the first cottage on the right from the main entrance of the carriageway to the Hall. His status in the daily running of the estate to the Hall, ranked alongside that of the Clerk of Works in seniority, sufficient for him to have his name listed in Kelly's commercial directory for Lincolnshire (Kelly`s Directories Ltd was a trade directory introduced in 1897 in the UK and listed all businesses & tradespeople in a particular County).

The facilities within the village, of some twenty odd dwellings, were at this time fairly primitive as compared to today's standards. There were no electricity therefore lighting by oil lamps and candles; open fires and ranges for cooking and warmth; coppers heated by burning solid fuels for hot water for washing clothes and supplying the transportable galvanised zinc bathtub with hot water by the bucket load and latrine facilities with the outside 'privy' and earth closet.

Ivy Cottage, the first on the right hand side, as viewed from the main carriage drive into Normanby Hall, North Lincolnshire, where Cyril was born and raised as a child.

Situated on the main street through the village was a Post Office opposite the main Estate Office and a school, built in 1864, which primarily consisted of two classrooms and a small playground. The school-master resided in his 'nominated' cottage within the village. Cyril and his elder brothers had a short walk to education as the school was situated next but one to their cottage.

Ernest and his wife Sarah Ann, who on the death of her father, Thomas Levis Green, on 28th May 1909, a resident of the village of Crosby, whose occupation was a builder and property owner, inherited a considerable portfolio of property and land in the villages of Scunthorpe, Frodingham, Ashby, Messingham and Barton upon Humber.

The rear garden at Ivy Cottage.
One of the Allen sons can be seen in the chicken run, with father, Ernest,
on the right hand pathway in the background

The family then moved from their Normanby cottage and purchased a property in the adjacent village of Burton upon Stather on the High Street, known as Central House. Built in the early part of the nineteenth century, the property supported a large parcel of land which ran from the rear of the house to the River Trent laid out with gardens, an orchard, housing for livestock and a plantain.

The family owned a horse and trap which was stabled on the property and, at the rear of the brick built house, was an adjoining two storey stone built cottage.

A family owned drapery business was established under the name of S Allen on Market Hill in Scunthorpe and managed by Cyril's two elder brothers Henry and Bertram. The business then became known as Allen Brothers.

The three brothers, Henry Levis, Bertram Green and Cyril Sheldon (now also known as Sid) moved into the living accommodation above the retail shop, whilst their sister, Marjorie (picture on left) remained living with her parents at Burton, Cyril also played football for the Market Hill Swifts.

Cyril (Sid), left front. Charity Football Match 1914 for the Market Hill 'Swifts'

It wasn't until 1908 that land between the villages of Crosby and Normanby was released by Sir Berkeley Sheffield for the open cast mining and smelting of iron ore. Evidence of iron smelting by the Romans had been found in various parts of North Lincolnshire.

An integrated iron and steel works was constructed on this land by John Lysaght Ltd, to supply steel for further processing at their Newport works, Wales. Commissioned in 1912, as well as the ore mines, the works consisted of ninety-six coke ovens, two blast furnaces (for producing 'pig iron') with a capacity of producing 700 tons per week, four 'open hearth' steel furnaces and steel rolling mills.

Cyril (Sid) joined the Mechanical Maintenance Department of the John Lysaght works during the commissioning stage, with a third blast furnace added to increase 'pig iron' capacity in 1913 an indicative expansion no doubt due to the deteriorating political situation in Continental Europe.

With the outbreak of war in 1914 the Allen brothers volunteered for service with the armed forces, with sister, Marjorie later joining the local Voluntary Aid Detachment (VAD's) nursing convalescing personnel sent from the Western Front, to a now converted military hospital at Normanby Hall.

Henry Levis (Harry) joined the Army Remount Service, whose task was to source and train horses and mules for military service in the cavalry and artillery, now known as 'Warhorses'.

Henry Allen training 'Warhorses'

Bertram Green (Bert) joined the Army Service Corps, motor transport section, and served in France and Flanders transporting personnel, goods and ordnance by motor lorry.

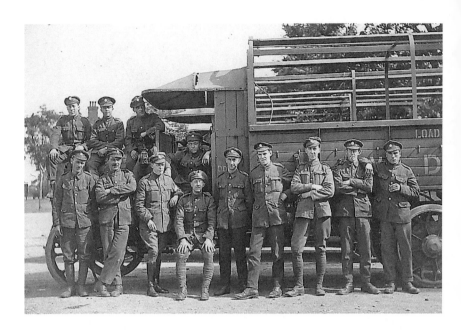

Bertram Allen ASC France (sat on lorry step)

Cyril Sheldon, no doubt from his skills in the 'mechanical world', was recruited into the Motor Machine Gun Service, administered by the Royal Artillery.

The family drapery business was consequently placed for sale by 'stock in trade' on 19th June 1915, by James Powell and Sons, Business Brokers, of Osborne Street, Hull.

Cyril sat astride an Army Douglas 2 ¾ HP (350cc) flat twin engine motorcycle, circa 1916

The house at Burton 99 years on (2015), the footpath and roadway levels were raised many years ago (By kind permission of Mr & Mrs Gill)

Normanby Hall, a view of the rear of the Hall taken from the grounds in 1908, note the new 'domestic' wing for the servants on the right hand side, built in 1907 and demolished in 1949

The front of the Hall and main entrance in 1909, the new servants 'domestic' wing is visible on the left.

Burton Hill as viewed from the Stather (derived from the Viking word staithes, a river landing) in 1913. The High Street is on the crest of the hill, the Allen property consisted of a long parcel of land which ran down to the banks of the River Trent

A postcard impression of John Lysaght's iron and steel-works in 1914, first commissioned in 1912, between the villages of Normanby and Crosby in North Lincolnshire

The Allen family Drapery business at 1, Market Hill, Scunthorpe was managed by brothers Henry and Bertram with, no doubt, Cyril being a 'silent partner' as he was employed in the mechanical engineers at Lysaght's Steelworks.

The three brothers occupied the accommodation above the retail shop. The business was sold when the three brothers decided to join the army.

Particulars of
SALE BY TENDER

OF THE

STOCK-IN-TRADE

OF

Messrs. Allen Brothers,

GENERAL DRAPERS,

SCUNTHORPE.

LINCOLNSHIRE.

On View upon the premises,

Market Hill,
SCUNTHORPE.

£458 0s. 11d.

SALE — June 19th, 1915.

TENDERS OPENED AT 11 O'CLOCK,

BY

JAMES POWELL & SONS,

Business Brokers,

Valuers, Fire Loss Assessors

and Stock Salesmen,

AT THEIR OFFICES,

27 to 45, Osborne Street, Hull.

Chapter 2   The Motor Machine Gun Service and MGC

At the outbreak of war in August 1914 the tactical use of machine guns was unappreciated by the British Army, who went to war with its infantry battalions and cavalry regiments each having a section of two machine guns. In the following November the Motor Machine Gun Service (MMGS) was formed, consisting of motor cycle mounted machine gun batteries.

After initial training Cyril was sent over to France but, similar to most of the men, Cyril and his brother Bertram, now in the Army Service Corps, had not been to France before and found themselves in a strange world. The Army, in its bid to attract men with knowledge of the 'internal combustion' engine and the riding of motorcycles, inserted recruiting adverts in magazines such as the 'Motor Cycle' on the home front.

Cyril (Sid) sat astride his Norton 490cc 'Brooklands Road Special', outside his parents' home at Burton upon Stather, 1916. (Note the belt drive to the rear wheel.) Wearing the uniform of the Motor Machine Gun Service

Cyril, no doubt by owning a Norton 490cc Brooklands Road Special, one of the fastest 'belt driven' machines of its day and with his civilian work experience in the mechanical engineering field, was welcomed as an ideal recruit. The MMGS was equipped with Vickers-Clyno motorcycle sidecar combination units, fitted with a Vickers Maxim machine gun on a specially adapted sidecar chassis, for rapid transport of the gun.

Men of the MMGS wore a different uniform with leather gaiters in place of puttees, goggles, gauntlets and in inclement conditions, weatherproof clothing for riding the machine, crash helmets were not issued. A khaki arm patch with the words Motor Machine Gun, picked out in red letters, was worn on the tunic shoulders.

Motor Machine Gun Service

The sidecar chassis, motorcycle frame, clutch and gearbox were manufactured by Clyno (other makes of motorcycle were also used), with an installed 750cc engine manufactured by Stevens Brothers. The initial idea of the combination units was for rapid deployment but, due to the rough terrain of battle worn ground and persistent water and mud, only limited use could be made of these machines. (The Service was withdrawn in the latter part of 1916)

A year of warfare on the Western Front proved that to be effective against the enemy, machine guns must be utilised in greater numbers by teams of specially trained men.

The Machine Gun Corps (MGC) was authorised by Army Orders on 14th October 1915 and was originally established in the Grantham area of Lincolnshire at Belton Park (Belton House) and in the grounds of Alma Park, known as Harrowby Camp. A training centre was later established at Wisques, south west of Calais, France on 22nd November 1915. Belton Park became home to over 170,000 members of the MGC from the infantry, cavalry and motors. The green grass of the parkland was soon replaced by a thousand huts, stables, chapels, a 670 bed military hospital and a railway which was a branch line north of Grantham from the East Coast main line operated by Great Northern Railways. The War Department operated its own loco, a Manning Wardle 0-4-0 shunting engine on the line, which was disused from 1922. Only physically fit and intelligent men were accepted into the Corps due to the weight of the equipment and technical knowledge required to fire and repair any consequential damage to the gun.

The Motors Branch, to which Cyril was attached, after absorbing the MMGS, formed various units consisting of motorcycle batteries, light car patrols and armoured cars manufactured by firms such as Rolls Royce, Austin, Lanchester, Wolseley etc.

Prior to this, some eighteen years earlier in 1897, Vickers, in Sheffield, Yorkshire, business of iron founders and steel armour plate manufacturers, purchased the automatic gun firm of Hiram

Maxim and Nordenfelt for £1.3million. Where previous designs of machine gun, such as the American Gatling, consisted of a number of barrels, which had to be rotated by hand cranking around a central shaft with a capability of firing 350 rounds per minute. The recoil from the firing action was classed as a necessary evil.

The Maxim (Vickers) gun was a truly automatic weapon, for the weapons recoil was turned to good account, by the means of inserting a new cartridge into the breach with a cyclic rate of fire of 450 rounds per minute of 0.303 inch calibre.

Overall the various branches of the MGC became known as 'The Suicide Club' due to the high casualty numbers in front line duty; 12,498 killed in action and 62,049 wounded (after the Great War in 1922, as a cost cutting exercise the MGC was disbanded).

Chapter 3   The Heavy Branch MGC and The Somme

The Heavy Branch of the Machine Gun Corps was formed during March 1916 then reformed into the Tank Corps on the 28th of July. Cyril was transferred to this Corps and assigned the 'trade' of Tank gunner. Each Tank was crewed by a 2nd Lieutenant, a commander, an NCO driver, two gears-men and four gunners.

A section of four Tanks was under the command of a Captain, four sections making up a Company under the command of a Major, and three Companies forming a Battalion under the command of a Lieutenant Colonel.

'A' Company was formed at Bisley in May 1916, and the Company moved to Elveden on Lord Iveagh's estate near Thetford, in June to train on the specially prepared training ground which was replicated with the broad and deep trenches as developed by the Germans at the Somme. Twenty five square miles of land had been developed into a specialist training facility for this innovative fighting machine. The land took in over seven farmsteads in the relatively deserted countryside of East Anglia,. The remoteness of the location also assisted the authorities in maintaining a 'tight web' of security around this new fighting machine.

The manufactured weight of the Tank, dependent on type, was over twenty seven tons, motorised lorries, in their infancy at this time, were not designed to carry such weights, so transportation of the Tanks had to be carried out on the railway network, not only in the home country, but also overseas on the battle-grounds. The Great Eastern Railway's Bury Saint Edmunds to Thetford line ran adjacent to Elveden, with stations at Thetford Bridge and nearby Barnham. A spur siding from the main line was constructed with a ramp to enable detraining of the Tanks for crew familiarisation training, then entraining for eventual shipment through Avonmouth Docks to France.

The accommodation at Elveden for other ranks was principally in tented camps with officers billeted in vacated farm buildings. The replica battlefield, in addition to the trenches, included wire entanglements, shell craters, machine gun emplacements, felled trees, emulating as realistically as possible the conditions expected at the Somme.

The Company was the third to deploy to France, the Tank crews leaving Southampton on the 14th of September for Le Havre, and then moving to the Somme where it reinforced C and D Companies during the Battle of Ancre.

On 15th September 1916, a new warfare technology appeared on the sodden battlefield of the Somme, the Tank. The offensive had been launched on 1st July and was in progress for nearly ten weeks with the allies advancing a depth of four miles of devastated countryside. With its origins in Lincoln, at the agricultural engineering works of William Fosters Ltd, the manufacture of the first 150 'Landships' happened in the space of six months (March to mid August) in absolute secrecy. The employees of Fosters were led to believe they were manufacturing large water-tanks for the Russian Government; the Tanks were not fitted with armaments at Foster's works. The army now had an armoured machine (the Mark I) that could traverse over unmade ground resilient to enemy gunfire. The Tanks fitted with 57mm (6 pounder) guns which were in short supply were known as 'males' and those with water cooled Vickers Maxim machine guns, a specially adapted version with raised foresights, as 'females'. The side 'capsules' on the Tanks were known as 'sponsons' where the main gunnery was installed.

The 'male' version of the Tank had a single 6 pounder gun in each sponson, with a large rear door which could be used in the event of escape if the Tank caught fire. This was totally the opposite to the 'female' Tank, where two machine guns were fitted in each sponson, with an arc of sweep of 180 degrees along each side of the Tank. Smaller sized doors were positioned below the sponson which resulted in these Tanks becoming virtual death traps for the crews if they caught fire during an attack.

The sponsons required unbolting for the Tanks transportation by rail, to reduce the overall width of the machine for the carriage movement through tunnels. Removing and the re-installation of the 'sponsons' was an arduous task, with each unit weighing 1 ton and 15 cwt (1.75t) and had to be manhandled and affixed with twenty six bolts.

The Mark I Tank required four men to drive it. There was a raised cupola at the front of the hull for the driver and commander who was also the 'brakes-man'. This gave a forward line of vision only and was protected by hinged flaps. The machine had an unwieldly two metal wheeled tail assembly, whose official name was a 'hydraulic stabiliser' which could be partly raised or lowered in the aid of steering the machine. This arrangement of steering on an Ackermann geometry axle, controlled by two 'Bowden cables' with steel wires, controlled by a steering wheel from the driving position was clumsy and laborious and wouldn't allow the machine to turn sharply on unmade ground. The engine and track assemblies required constant attention, with the idler rollers which were positioned along the underside length of the track frame being an everlasting source of trouble.

The fuel tanks containing petroleum spirit were mounted high in the rear hull giving a gravity feed of fuel to the engine, which could result in fuel starvation on steep inclines, in addition to being a fire risk.

Cyril took part in this first advance of the Tanks with 'A' Company and was despatched to the Yvrench training centre in France. Here trenches had been dug and wire entanglements erected, and machine gun and 6-pounder practice could be carried out in a fashion. But there was no staff of instructors. The firing ranges were too short, and the conditions for battle practice were quite unlike those that prevailed on the Somme.

When moving up to the forward area there were endless lines of transport crawling over incredibly bad road surfaces bordered by gaunt stumps of trees and by a sordid and tragic litter of dead men, horses, rags, tin cans, rotting equipment and derelict transport.

When going into battle, from a list drawn up by Captain Henriques, the problems of 'house-keeping' inside each Tank became problematic. With a crew of eight, each man carried two gas helmets and one pair of goggles, in addition to their ordinary service caps and a leather 'anti- bruise' helmet. Other equipment consisted of a large field and ordinary first aid dressings, a revolver, haversack, water bottles and iron rations. In addition to this, sixteen loaves of bread, some thirty tins of food, cheese, tea, sugar and milk were also added.
Bread loaves were issued as an antidote to carbon monoxide (CO) poisoning from exposure to the exhaust fumes, which led to drowsiness and a desire to sleep as it absorbs oxygen in the bloodstream.

Additional maintenance items included a spare drum of engine oil and one of gear oil, two small drums of grease, three water-cans and two boxes of revolver ammunition, 33,000 rounds of machine gun ammunition, four spare Vickers MG barrels, one spare Vickers gun, a spare Hotchkiss gun barrel and two wire cutters.

Many Tanks also carried two carrier pigeons for delivering messages from the Tank. The birds had to be released before sunset so as not to break their journey home to the loft by roosting on the way. Also included were a lamp and flag signalling sets, a portable field telephone set with one hundred yards of cable spooled from a drum as the Tank traversed forward, relating its experiences to a person at the rear. (Later, at the 3rd Battle of Ypres, each Tank was also issued with a brass carriage clock, six periscopes and an electric hand-lamp.) Trials of early wireless systems for use in Tanks were not carried out until May 1917 at the Central Workshops in Erin, France.

Whilst the time of day was all important in engaging the enemy, the common type of timepiece was the pocket watch, which was cumbersome in tunic pockets for quick timing decisions. This led to the further development and use of the wristlet watch which was little used by the sterner sex before the war, but was now much sought after by the man in uniform. Officers were personally required to provide some of their own equipment, and wristlet watches, with recently introduced luminous dials, were advantageous in areas of darkness or restricted daylight especially in the Tanks.

The luminous dials and hands of a watch were spot coated with radium luminous paint which was made by mixing radium salts and zinc sulphide in a 'binder' of clear varnish. The radium gives off alpha particles which can't be seen by the naked eye, but when they hit the zinc sulphide it causes them to give off a flash of light. This gradually wears out as the zinc sulphide gives a luminous effect for a three year life, but the radium which has a half-life of around 1,600 years, remains fully radio-active.

'A' Company, commanded by Major C M Tippetts arrived in France too late to take part in the Battle of Flers-Courcelette. His ten Tanks were supposed to support the 18th Division in their thrust on the Ancre Heights. Orders spelt out in a divisional instruction G391, dated 23rd October 1916, were a demanding one, for it involved an advance of over 2750 metres, just to reach South Miraumont Trench and further on the village of Petit Miraumont, the way was barred with trenches, wire, deep mud and a shelled terrain.

With all these groups of Mark 1 Tanks, the preliminary moving up to first line positions with a maximum speed of 4 mph, in the pitch dark, through mud (although the weight imposition through the 'self-laying' roadway was 10½lbs/ sq inch [0.738 kg/ sq cm] to the ground, which is not excessive to culverts under surfaced road-ways) and avoiding shell holes, proved most arduous, putting a tremendous strain on both men and officers. The crews then spent the rest of the night adjusting the centrally mounted Daimler 105hp (78.3Kw) petrol engine, which had a two speed gear-box with a differential drive to two cross shafts connected to the rear driving sprockets by roller chain drive and reduction gears. Between the Daimler engine and gear-box was a platform for four of the crew to crank the engine starting handle, two each side.

Lubricating the 'running gear' associated with the track assemblies consisted of 72 greasing points around the outside of the Tank. The type of grease point in use at this time, consisted of a threaded plug which had to be removed from the end of a roller. A screwed connecting pipe was inserted, to inter-connect the barrel of the grease gun which was pressurised by a screwing action, not a pleasant task. Inside the Tank were 21 grease cups which had to be filled with grease, then screwed down tight. Track-pad and drive chain tension had also to be adjusted whilst listening to the explosions of the British artillery bombardment.

Of the 52 Tanks available for operation assembled behind lines at Acheux, 20 Tanks were allocated to II Corps and 32 to V Corps.

The employment of Tanks in this their first series of battles had been essentially experimental but, to our own infantry, the Tank appeared as a lusty friend who had found a way of dealing with the partnership of enemy barbed wire and machine gun fire.

To the Tank crews, the events of the day were probably viewed somewhat in deference, after being half choked with engine fumes, enclosed for many hours without respite in the intolerable clamour, restriction of space, high levels of noise and temperature, shaking and movement of the travelling machine, along with gun and shell fire. Crews were issued with chain mail face masks, to offer protection from metal spatter from the Tank hull when being hit by enemy gun fire.

After the experiences that the Tanks gained on the Somme, it was decided to expand the Corps from four Companies to four Battalions. This was carried out in France and orders were issued to 'A' Company to withdraw from the forward area to billets in and around Humieres on 18th November 1916. Owing to unforeseen circumstances 'A' Company was unable to entrain until the 30th November and did not arrive at Wavrans until the early hours of 1st December. The Company was divided into three parts in the railway station yard, one to proceed to Humerouille, the other two to Humieres and Eclimeux, where they formed the No's 1,2 and 3 Companies of 'A' Battalion.

During December, reinforcements of officers and other ranks were constantly arriving and work was mainly concentrated in improving conditions in the camps. Local training was carried out until new Tanks arrived during February 1917, and a new Tankodrome was erected at Eclimeux. During March, intensive training was carried out and included revolver practice, toxic gas drill, operating in gas helmets, machine gun and cannon training.

No 3 Company moved from Eclimeux on the 20th May and entrained at Erin on the 21st, followed by No2 on the 23rd, and No1 on the 24th. Battalion HQ was moved by lorry on the 25th to Ouderdom Camp where accommodation was under canvas. Hangars were erected at the Tankodrome to secure the Mark VI Tanks from aerial observation. The strength of the Battalion on the 31st of May was 90 officers and 668 other ranks.

Chapter 4   The Battle for Messines

The Battle for Messines was a limited offensive designed to capture the Messines Ridge and secure the high ground on the right flank for the main offensive on Ypres. Heavy artillery bombardment of the German lines commenced on the 21st May 1917, involving 2,300 guns and 300 heavy mortars. Tanks of No 2 and 3 Companies moved a distance of about 4 miles towards the front line on June 4th 1917, parked up the Tanks and returned to camp by motor lorry. On the following day, they were joined by No 1 Company. The three Companies then progressed a further 4 miles to the laying up point with the following day being taken as a rest day. The artillery bombardment ceased at 02:50 hours on June 7th and silence prevailed from the British lines for twenty minutes.

Zero hour for No 2 and 3 Companies, using their full complement of Tanks, was at 3-10am on June 7th, No 1 Company was in reserve. The battle opened in what was the finest barrage of the war. A special action to be mentioned was the blowing up of nineteen out of twenty-one land mines containing over a million pounds of ammonal under the enemy's front line. This was to be the signal for the attack. Some of the mines had been ready for more than a year, with the tunnelling companies of the Royal Engineers constructing more than five miles of galleries.

At zero hour, a low rumbling was heard; the earth rocked and quivered until, with a prolonged and rending crash, a screen of fire rose where the German front lines had been. Masses of earth were hurled skywards and balls of fire flew in every direction and the air quivered, the ground vibrating with the shock.
Altogether 72 Mark IV Tanks were employed, with 12 Mark I and Mark II Tanks being converted into supply machines as they were

able to bring up sufficient petrol, ammunition and other stores to replenish five fighting Tanks.

The Mark IV was a much improved engineered version of the Mark I, and did not differ in shape and dimension, but improvements included better quality steel plate on the 'hull' to resist enemy armour piercing ordnance. Other improvements concerned the self-laying roadway of crawler tracks, with a heavier design of track idler rollers and crawler belt pad-plates, the removal of the petrol tank to the rear of the machine protected under armour plating. The 'sponsons' which housed the guns were re-engineered to enable them to be partially retracted into the main hull of the Tank when being transported on rail cars. This was an improvement on the Mark I, where the' sponsons' required removal for shipment by rail. Other minor improvements concerned the armament.

No 3 Company 'A' Battalion with the 41st and 47th Divisions, X Corps, 2nd Army, intended to get 12 Tanks into action, four from each of Sections 10, 11 and 12, supported by two Supply Tanks from Section 9.

It is presumed that Cyril was in 11 Section under the command of Captain D T Raikes, crewing Tank A55 Se 2666 'Revenge' (later to be officially renamed 'Aggressive') under the command of 2[nd]Lt J L Loveridge.

The Tanks, each carrying two pigeons for sending information back, moved off to their various objectives on a line running approximately east of the village of Oosttaverne. Many ditched because of the cohesive ground, but rapidly overcame their difficulties and followed up the attack at full speed, reaching a ridge overlooking the enemy who were now in full retreat. The enemy repeatedly attempted to advance, raking the Tanks with a hail of armour piercing 'K' bullets, which failed to penetrate the 'plated' hull of the Mark IV.

The four Tanks of 11 Section starting at Zero hour (3:10 am) reached Eikhof Farm at 4:45 am. The Tanks then split into pairs, after half an hour, A55 'Revenge' and A54, Se 2003, 'Iron Rations' (later to be officially renamed 'Adsum') crossed the Dammestrasse, briefly ditching, then caught up with the barrage and joined the infantry as they advanced and crossed the Black Line, turning right and proceeded along the edge of Denis Wood before sighting targets down Obstacle Avenue.

At 3:05pm, both Tanks supported the attack on the Green Line and went down Obscure Alley progressing to Rose Wood and crossing the Roozebeck on the way to Green Wood where they engaged the enemy. A55 'Revenge' fired Lewis guns at the enemy infantry and machine gunners in and around the Wood, then turned north following the ravine to Verhaest Farm along the northern edge of Rose Wood to Obscure Alley and rallying.

The following morning the enemy counter attacked but the Tanks repelled this attack until the arrival of further support. The outcome of the battle was one of the most successful that was ever fought. The captures amounted to 7,300 prisoners, 67 artillery guns, 94 trench mortars and a very large number of machine guns.

The Battle of Messines, one of the shortest and best mounted limited operations of the war, was in no sense a Tank battle, the success being rightly credited to the tunnelling company. Tanks took but a small part in it, except in its final stages but, nevertheless, many useful strategic lessons on their use were learnt.

On the evening of the 9th of June, all the Tanks were withdrawn to the 'Tankodrome', where all the necessary repairs were carried out and reinforcements received, and on the 14th the GOC. Major General Elles, DSO, inspected the Battalion.

'A' Battalion, synonymous with the other Tank Battalions adopted official names preceded by the Battalions letter. This occurred between the Battles of Messines and 3rd Ypres on July 31st.

Chapter 5   Means of Communication

Before the introduction of the wartime invention of the Tank, most of the war had been fought from reasonably static positions, such as the trench system devised by both sides. Communications to the 'back office' at headquarters could be made by installed cable systems, which were dependent on location either installed underground such as at the front, or overhead on a more permanent basis referred to as air-line. Some tens of thousands of miles of copper cored cables were laid behind the trenches, inter-connecting headquarters (HQ) with the frontline itself.

The equipment used on these systems consisted of electro-magnetic sounders (receiver) activated at the other end of the line by a telegraph sending key (transmitter) using the Morse telegraph code. Since the systems operated on low voltage batteries such as Leclanche cells, various circuits such as double current systems were devised to counter 'voltage drop' over long distances.

Development of the 'field telephone' system was also important. It is applied as we know, more particularly to the sound waves which constitute human speech, and the telephone allows us to transmit them over considerable distance by land-lines in the form of variable electrical currents, which are again converted back into sound waves at the receiving end. However, due to using a single conductor wire and earth, it became possible for the enemy in laying lengths of wire along their forward trenches to act as aerials (antennae), which could intercept telegraph and telephone messages by induction through the soil. Further development of this was integrated into the 'Fullerphone', which initially was a telegraph system which transmitted DC signals through a single wire and earth but incorporated a 'scrambler' system, later being applied to telephone messages.

Until towards the end of 1916, there was no reliable means of communication between Tanks at the front and headquarters during an attack or, from Tank to Tank, or, Tank to accompanying infantry or aircraft. On September 11th the first instructions relating to Tank signalling were issued, which were from Tank to infantry or aircraft as follows:-

Flag Signals:
Red flag .... Out of action
Green flag .... Closing on objective

Lamp Signals:
A Series of Morse T's (dashes)........... Out of action
A Series of Morse H's (dots) .... Closing on objective

Semaphore discs:
Coloured discs hoisted on a topside fixed pole,
useful for inter-tank and infantry signals.

The use of these systems was fairly limited on account of the dense smoke clouds caused by the guns and the incoming enemy bursting shell-fire.

The use of men trained as message Runners between the front and HQ were also another form of battle communication, but unfortunately many were caught up in the conditions of the conflict itself and finished up at best as casualties.

Most Tanks ordered into action carried a basket containing at least two homing pigeons. A trained handler within the crew would attach a small capsule containing a paper message to one of the bird's legs, and the bird's release from the Tank would be by a small aperture engineered on one of the sponsons. Many London type motor omnibuses were converted to mobile pigeon lofts, for use of receiving the birds and attached messages for dissemination by headquarters staff some distance behind the lines of the battle front. The pigeons were fairly reliable if they could be kept intact until needed, taking into account the conditions within the Tank, excess heat from the engine and fired ordnance, exhaust gases such as carbon monoxide and cordite gases from ordnance and noise levels in excess of 130 Decibels.

It should be appreciated by the reader that only twenty years before the Great War, in 1894, the world's first public demonstration of wireless was made by Sir Oliver Lodge at Oxford in August, based on the work of his late friend Heinrich Hertz, who had passed away on the 1st of January. The technology developed was based on high voltage sparks which took place between polished, hemisphere shaped electrodes, tuned by Leyden Jars and connected to aerial and an earth electrode, this work being further developed by the Marconi Company.

The Army, in adopting wireless technology, lagged behind the Navy who had recently commissioned Wireless Station, Cleethorpes, Lincolnshire, with the most powerful transmitter in the world along with an installation in Gibraltar, and also the Royal Flying Corps. The RFC standard airborne equipment in 1914 was the 'Sterling' spark gap transmitter, powered from 10 volt accumulators. The transmitters output of 30 – 40 Watts fed to the 120 feet (36.9M) of trailing aerial wire which gave it an operating range of 8 – 10 miles. The aerial of stranded copper wire with a 3lb (1.2Kg) weight on the end was wound out from a spool through an insulated gland in the floor of the aircraft; the operator in the aircraft had no receiver. The role of 'observer' aircraft was to direct the gunfire of artillery batteries below, via morse code signals received on a reception set, under the control of an RFC TunerWireless Operator attached to each battery. The Ground

Wireless Operators were equipped with several strips of white cloth for use when signalling back to the overhead aircraft, laid out on the ground in a coded pattern or a morse signalling lamp.

Similar wireless systems consisting of portable 'Trench Sets', which worked off the spark induction coil principle of transmission, was employed in the forward areas by the Army. These had a limited range of transmission from a thousand to four thousand yards, dependent on the aerial height erected as long as it remained there due to enemy shelling. Therefore with the introduction of the travelling Tank to the battle front, as opposed to the fixed concrete German 'Pill Boxes' containing machine guns, communications back to staff from their forward positions was becoming a problem as nothing more was heard of them until the attack had quietened down or, they had returned to their rallying positions.

Reception, or Tuners as they were referred to, worked with a Carborundum or Perikon crystal detector. Successful reception required an aerial of 100 to 125 feet length (30 metres plus) supported on 15 ft high (4.6 metres) masts.

This state of affairs had to be remedied in the battle zone. This manifested itself at Tank Corps HQ where twenty four men were selected and sent to the Royal Engineers wireless school to learn the Morse code and the operation and maintenance of spark and continuous wave (CW) transmitters and crystal and thermionic valve (tube) receivers. Most of the trainee operators attained a sending speed in the Morse code of twenty five words per minute by the conclusion of the six week course. The continuous wave (CW) transmitter was issued to the Tanks in the spring of 1918 as it was more dependent for its operation with thermionic valves, being more compact and offered greater range with smaller aerials.

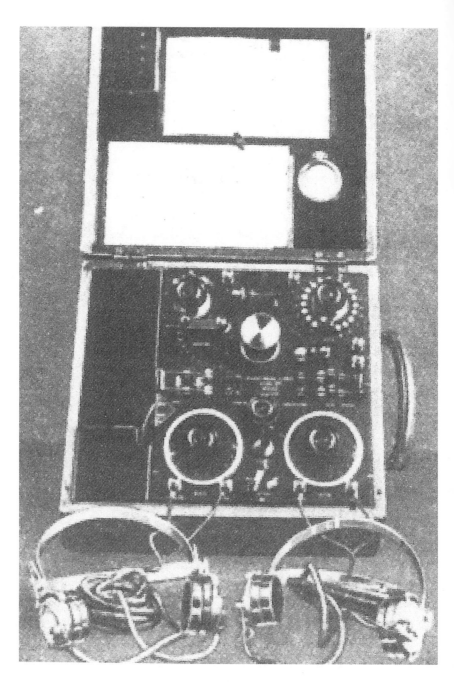

Short Wave 'Tuner' MK III "Crystal Detector"

From the wireless school the trained operators were sent to the Tank Corps, Central Workshops at Erin, France, where six female Mark 1 Tanks were in the process of having machine guns removed from their sponsons, which were in turn converted into a wireless telegraphy office and the other sponson utilised for the stowage of the equipment. An aerial mast which could be lowered was installed on the forward top-side of the Tank.

The Wireless Tanks were moved up to the Ypres Salient by train, just clearing the bridges by 6 inches (150 mm). On arrival at their destination the Tanks were hidden in the woods. Many days were spent preparing for action; charging accumulators, checking receivers, but the transmitter kept silent so as not to alert the enemy of any forthcoming action. The modified fighting machines with a hinged aerial mast which could be raised to a height of at least two and half times the height of the Tank to support two spreaders from a 'T' piece for the multiple 'caged' aerial wires, must have caught the imagination of Gunner Cyril S Allen and his fellow 'Tankies', who were now witnessing the use of electro-technology for the first time in an armoured fighting vehicle.

On the evening of July 30th, two Wireless Tanks, deployed by C and F Battalions, moved up to the front line of fighting Tanks and, at zero hour the following morning, moved forward just behind the infantry, and remained static whilst 'on air'. The first use of these Wireless Tanks was in itself somewhat of a failure. "No one knew why they were there, or, in fact knew that there were such things as Wireless Tanks. We kept in contact with our directing station ten miles away and were ready at any minute to deal with messages, but none was forthcoming", from the words of one of the wireless operators.

A " WIRELESS " TANK.

Later use of the Wireless Tanks in various parts of the Ypres salient justified itself when communications were made full use of, but it was quickly realised that if the Tank itself was put out of action either with mechanical problems or being hit by a shell, the fixed wireless apparatus was useless. A retro-fit was then carried out to remount the apparatus in a portable form in a cabinet so that the apparatus could quickly be removed bodily when the occasion required it.

Two 30 foot (9.05Metres) steel masts were carried for use when the apparatus was used in portable form in 'dug-outs' or enemy concrete 'pill boxes' which were in plentiful number in the Menin district. Evidently they made excellent wireless stations but with little protection for the elevated aerial (antenna) system.

The wireless technology of the time was based on the 'spark transmitter', every spark station having its own characteristic sound and any aerial of a height of less than 30 feet made working signals at a twenty mile range impossible. Therefore the erected aerials became very conspicuous and were, in the recollections of a wireless operator, "a record if one lasted ten minutes intact, before being blown away by enemy gunfire".

Operators engaged in the repair of the double wire aerial which, at first, was made of 7/22 (7 strands of 22 gauge) copper wire, had a very busy and risky time, often with the masts having to be repaired with 'splints' improvised from barbed wire stakes, whilst under enemy gunfire.

On 20th September 'A' Battalion, No 8 Section, No 2 Company, under Captain A J Skelding, sent two wireless equipped Tanks forward with the 1st Australian and 41st Divisions ANZAC and X Corps 2nd Army. The Wireless Tank working with the ANZAC's was ordered to establish a signal station at the SW corner of

Glencourse Wood, one and a half hours after zero. The one working with X Corps was to establish a signal station at the west edge of Clonmel Copse. Two wireless operators were provided to each tank, 2nd Lt J Evans being attached to the Section as Wireless Officer. The Tank at Glencourse Wood, successfully remained on station for 24 hours, under very heavy shellfire.

On the 26th of September, Captain J Fitzmaurice established a wireless station between Glencourse and Polygon Woods. Although coming under the enemy counter barrage, he remained on station for over 36 hours. Now the Wireless Tanks were being made full use of, and the experiment of using mobile wireless stations at the fighting front had justified itself.

After Ypres, and further intensive training in signals, the next use of the Wireless Tanks was the Battle of Cambrai in the following November, where nine machines were allocated, one to each Tank Corps Battalion. In this battle wireless signalling proved invaluable in keeping in touch with the 'back office' (HQ) and also sending communications forward to the battle front. The wireless stations were positioned at least 500 yards behind the fighting Tanks, and the officer in charge of this forward station would compile periodic message reports for the telegraphy operators to transmit to headquarters.

Chapter 6   The 3rd Battle of Ypres

The 2nd Brigade (A and B Tank Battalions) were then moved by seven trains on to a new camp at Ouderdom, followed on the 25th June by Battalion HQ, in preparation for the 3rd Battle of Ypres. Intense training was now started, as was reconnaissance for the big attack for what was planned at the end of July.

On the 5th of July, a new un-ditching system was issued to the Battalion. This consisted of a substantial hardwood beam somewhat greater than the width of the Tank over its tracks and therefore it was carried length-wise along the back of the machine, but in its battle position, carried laterally on the topside of the Tank hull on two rails. When engaged, by connecting chains to the pads on the left and right hand track frames, this teak baulk, iron shod at the ends, could be propelled under the tracks, to assist adhesion for self-recovery from a shell hole. When the Tank became 'bellied' the drag chains had to be attached by a crew member climbing out onto the roof - a no mean feat in the near presence of the enemy. With the beam being attached, the differential gear locked and the clutch released, the revolving tracks would carry the beam over the nose of the Tank until dragged beneath the Tank itself. This addition was to prove extremely useful later on the water logged ground surrounding Ypres, which was practically all reclaimed swamp land.

All agriculture in this area depended on careful drainage. The country in this part of Flanders is flat and swampy - the water being carried away in innumerable dykes. So important was the maintenance of these, that in normal times, a farmer who allowed them to fall into disrepair was heavily fined. A hundred years earlier, Ypres had been a seaport, but land had been reclaimed from the sea by an intricate system of drainage dykes. Across this terrain two armies had faced each other for nearly three years with constant shelling of the low ground blocking the dykes and natural drainage, turning the ground into a sodden wilderness.

Yet it was across this type of ground that the infantry was to attack, and for some unknown reason from the High Command, heavy Tanks were chosen to assist them. Senior officers in the Tank Brigades protested vehemently that no Tank could cross such water-logged ground and, if they were used, it would simply be throwing away highly trained men and wasting valuable machines. But the decree had gone forth. The High Command was intent on its battle and it had been ordained that Tanks should be used. Arguments about the ground conditions were to no avail.

The Germans were firmly seated in a semi-circle on a ridge of low hills which overlooked Ypres and the British lines from three different directions. Behind the enemy lines was a swampy valley and toward the rear of that, another low ridge of hills. The objectives of the High Command was to attack across the marshy ground, capture the first line of hills, descend into the swamp on the other side, then advance uphill, to storm the second ridge.

Week by week, the concentration of allied troops and their equipment increased. The enemy observed it all with great interest. They shelled every road, railway and wooded areas where troops could shelter with overnight bombing by aircraft on huts and dug outs. Allied working parties had to work during the darkness of the night digging gun pits, trenches, constructing causeways and duckboard tracks. Every night and all night enemy shelling took place and many lives were lost but the allies stuck grimly to their task. The methodical habits of the Germans even extended to their shelling, with intervals of ten minutes, where the allies dashed hastily across the danger zone, before the next batch of shells was due to arrive.

The enemy had for long been in no doubt about the Allies intentions and had devised a new tactical method - the use of a comparatively new contrivance - the 'pill-box', a small reinforced concrete fort with some one metre thick walls. Sometimes it only stood a metre or two above the ground level or was concealed in derelict farms. It held a garrison of 30 to 40 men, plentifully supplied with loop-holes through which to point the noses of machine guns. The ordinary high explosive shell 'thrown' by a field gun having little effect on them.

The Allies Reconnaissance Officers had been busy during the weeks of preparation for the battle, through June and early July. From a mass of gathered information, a huge sand model of Ypres Salient was laid out by the 19th Corps in Oosthoek Wood. The aspect of a salient is a piece or neck of ground projecting into the enemy lines and offering disadvantages and dangers to the defenders. Every hillock, depression, road, railway, stream, trench and other landmark was reproduced to scale, with the model covering nearly an acre. At one side a raised viewing platform was erected where both Tank commanders and Infantry officers with whom they were to fight, could 'walk and talk' over the ground together. As most of the landmarks had disappeared the Recce Officers set out to map out a series of compass bearings to points within the enemy's lines.

For Tanks to move up to the line across the countryside of dykes and swamps, it was necessary to construct miles of causeways and bridges over canals. This work was carried out in full view of the Germans who rained down high explosive shells containing shrapnel and also gas shells. This work was valiantly carried out by the 184th Tunnelling Company of Royal Engineers. They often toiled away with mud up to their knees, compelled to wear gas masks for long periods. After successfully laying a stretch of causeway, they then often saw it destroyed in a matter of minutes by enemy shelling.

On 17th July, the Fifth Army attack on the enemy was to be carried out on well recognised lines, namely a lengthy artillery preparation followed by an infantry attack on a large scale that utilised three Brigades of Tanks; the 2nd Army Corps employing the 2nd Tank Brigade (A and B Btn's) to the 24, 30, 18, 8 and 25th divisions. The general objective was the capture of the Broodseinde ridge and the protection of the right flank of the Fifth Army. A and B Battalions were allocated 72 Tanks for this offensive to be carried out over a 7 mile length of a 15 mile Front, zero hour commencing at 3:30am on 31 July 1917. No 3 Company had 12 Tanks in action and the Allies gained their objectives practically everywhere.

It was probable that Gunner C S Allen was a crew member of Tank A55, Se 2666, 'Aggressive' under the command of 2ndLt J L Loveridge, of Section 11, which was commanded by Captain D T Raikes. The other Tanks in the Section were A52 Se 2670 'Artful Alice', A53 Se2680 'Angelina' and A54 Se2003 'Adsum'. The orders and objectives for Section 11 in the line of attack were to support the 24th Brigade on the right with the 2nd East Lancs and the 1st Sherwood Forresters on the left and only operate in attack if the infantry were held up. If the attack was successful the Section was then to take up positions behind the 'Black Line' to repel any forthcoming counter attacks. The Tank A54 reached the British Front Line and was knocked out by shell fire. A53 crossed the German Front Line, ditched and broke down. A52 almost reached the Black Line and along with A55 passed through the infantry to attack enemy machine guns which were stopping the advance, A52 was then knocked out after becoming hit six times by enemy gun-fire.

A55 'Aggressive' became ditched on the Black Line, the crew dismounted into shell holes from where they fired over 3,000 rounds of small arms ammunition breaking up an enemy counter attack. The Tank was then un-ditched using the un-ditching beam recovered from A52, then went on to recover guns and stores from the other knocked out Tanks within the Section. Whilst returning to the rallying point A55 was hit by an enemy shell. In the aftermath, No 3 Company did not see action again as a unit at Ypres and A55 'Aggressive' was probably unfit for further use as no record exists of this machine after this date. 'Aggressive' was replaced later by 'Aggressive II' A55 Se 2878 at Cambrai.

An enemy all night artillery barrage on August 1st and rain falling at the rate of 25mm for the following four days, resulted in the undrained land becoming a swamp. The few defined tracks became targets for the enemy's artillery, shell holes consequently becoming ponds. Many of the Tanks 'bellied' in boggy ground. Some, by use of their un-ditching beams, managed to struggle out of the oozing slime. The majority sunk lower and lower until water entered through the sponson doors and stopped the engine. As they wallowed in the mud they were attacked by aircraft and artillery fire, with many of the crews being wounded or killed before engaging with the enemy. It was nearly a fortnight before the Fifth Army could again attack. The disappointment of the Higher Command was acute. The Commander of the Fifth Army subsequently based a generally unfavourable report upon the Tanks.

On August 22nd, a minor attack was launched by all three Corps, each making use of a small number of Tanks, with the 2nd Corps in Glencourse Wood, four Tanks of the 2nd Brigade were of some service with some considerable execution. The main problem with all ongoing operations was the condition of the ground. Any Tank that ventured to leave a roadway, in such condition as they were after heavy shelling, would instantly belly in the quagmire of mud and water, often being one to two metres deep. General Elles, in view of these appalling ground conditions, had originally estimated that one machine in two would engage in effective action but subsequently revised this estimate to one in ten engaging the enemy.

On the following day, four 2nd Brigade Tanks went into action near Inverness Copse, the operation was undertaken in a hurry with poor liaison and the attack was a failure. Some three weeks elapsed before Tanks were again in action with several Battalions of the 2nd and 3rd Brigades being moved to a new training ground near Arras.

September the 20th saw a reasonably successful assault made along the whole line, with the 2nd Brigade taking a minor part near Inverness Copse due to the appalling ground condition. Trees had been felled across the roadways by the enemy, resting high on their branches and tall stumps from which the trunk had not been completely severed, formed a barrier creating a formidable task for the crews to get to the battle. If a leading machine got into difficulties along the narrow hardened foundations of the roadway, the whole line of following Tanks would be held up due to the deep swamps on either side.

October the 4th saw the last two actions of this battle in which Tanks succeeded in playing a part. The first was by twelve Tanks of the 1st Brigade who took part in the capture of Poelcapelle. Whilst the idea of Tanks on the battlefield was wallowing in the gloomy 'Slough of Despond', the second battle showed a great feat of heroism shining out over the marshy wastes like a beacon. Four Tanks of the 1st ('A') Battalion took part in an attack upon Juniper Cottage on the line of the Reutel-beek.

As the condition of the ground was bad, Captain Clement Robertson, Officer Commanding No 12 Section, 'A' Battalion, set out accompanied by Gunner Cyril S Allen, No 11 Section No 3 Company 'A' Battalion, who had volunteered to assist to tape out a route for another Section commander. They followed a pre-determined route. The vision available to Tank commanders and drivers was very limited with forward vision only, so any surrounding landmarks were probably not observed for guidance. Working all night and with very little sleep during the day, this task occupied them from September 30th to October 3rd. On October the 1[st,] Gunner Allen had been blown off his feet by a falling enemy exploding shell burst, which flung showers of mud and debris over him and he was severely shaken. This occurred whilst assisting in the reeling out and the laying down of marker tapes of a route from Observatory Ridge to Polygon Wood. But with great determination he stuck to his self-imposed duty.

The reason for the use of the white marker tapes was that the overall external visual aspect for the driver and commander from within the Tank was very limited. The condition of the terrain over which the Tanks were required to travel was one of deep mud pitted with craters from enemy shells and debris. Once it had started out over `No Man`s Land` the Tank was a self-contained unit, the commander and crew were cut off from the outside world in their narrow iron clad machine. Communication to individual Tanks was limited to observe any visual signals given from the exterior. Wireless as it was developed at this time was not installed in individual Tanks. If surrounded by the enemy, there was no appealing by the Tank commander to a higher authority for support.

It wasn't until 9-30pm on October 3rd that the Captain and Cyril had plotted out and taped a satisfactory route from Polygon Wood to Blackwatch Corner. A heavy enemy barrage was encountered but they continued in laying the tape running from shell hole to shell hole. Without a break they both went forward on foot leading the Tanks to their starting point safely by 3:00am on October 4th. They both rested for a couple of hours until 6:00am when, through the early morning mist, the Captain decided to lead his Tanks (A56 female, A58 male, A59 male, A60 female) into action on foot to prevent them missing the narrow bridge which crossed a stream known as the Reutel-beek. The ground had suffered an intense bombardment, trees, hedges and roads had disappeared but, by some strange chance, the small bridge had remained.

If the Tanks, blundering from one muddy crater to the next, failed to see the bridge, the action was lost, so Captain Robertson, assisted by Gunner Allen, guided them to the other side of the stream. The German barrage came down furiously, rifles cracked and machine guns spluttered but the two lone figures progressed steadily forward. They were now ahead of the infantry and, in Cyril's own words, "had not many yards to go before reaching enemy lines, and coming face to face with the Boche" Cyril continues, "Captain Robertson still went on, whilst I went behind to guide our last Tank up and, no sooner had I returned to the front again, to my surprise I am sorry to say the Captain was missing. At this time we were under heavy machine gun and rifle fire which, on being that intense, I had to creep on my hands and knees, and not many yards away I found Captain Robertson laying in a small shell hole wounded. All I can say is that I did my very best for him, as it should be, and held him in my arms until he died".

The former words of Cyril's are extracts from a letter that he wrote on the battlefield to the late Captain's mother, but unfortunately the letter was never sent from the front in the Army Postal Service, due to Cyril himself being killed in action some six weeks later. From the text of the letter Cyril states, "I have been with him on several such occasions and know his worth. I thereupon let the tanks successfully career on to their objectives, as owing to us being in 'no man's land' it was impossible for me to have his body put on a Tank, so I took what effects off him as I could possibly get, atlas maps, papers, etc," to prevent them entering enemy hands.

Cyril then arose from the shell hole and staggered to the friendly shelter of the nearest Tank, which then successfully drove the enemy from their strong positions. On completion of the action, he reported the Captain's death to HQ and returned his maps and papers. For their gallant efforts Captain C Robertson was posthumously awarded the Victoria Cross (VC) and Cyril Sheldon for his true grit and determination in the field of battle, the Distinguished Conduct Medal (DCM).

Orders were received on the 8th that the Battalion was to move to Wailly on the 11th, and two trains were allocated for this purpose, the first leaving at 2:00 am and the second at 11:00am. Headquarters moved by road on the 13th and, by noon on the 14[th,] the move was complete.

Footnote: Captain C Robertson promoted from 2nd Lt was the commander of Tank A56 Se2692 at the Battle of Messines and crossed the German Front Line until hit by a 6 inch shell injuring two crew members and killing the Sergeant and causing damage to one of the 'sponsons'. The Tank was returned to Central Workshops and returned to action in February 1918.

King George V and Brigadier General Hugh Elles, of the Tank Corps,
watch a demonstration of two new Mark IV Tanks during July 1917.
Note the 'female' on the left and the 'male' on the right
which is indicative of their armaments.

Mark IV Tanks at a railhead before the Battle of Cambrai.
They are equipped with fascines for crossing the trenches, un-ditching beams
and their sponsons are swung inwards for rail travel.

A 'Carte Postale' sent home to England by Sid to his family

A photograph sent home of some of Cyril's fellow 'Tankies', names not known.
All are wearing the Tank badge on the right tunic sleeve.

Chapter 7   The Battle of Cambrai

On October 20th, the project for the battle was approved and its date fixed for November the 20[th.] The battle was to be based on Tanks and led by them without any preliminary bombardment of the artillery. The Tanks on this date were scattered over a considerable area; some were at Ypres, Lens and others at Bermicourt. These would all have to be assembled at various training areas so that cooperative training with the infantry could take place. This was of importance, as confidence in the infantry in the tanks was as important as the surprise attack itself. The attack was to rely upon surprise, audacity and rapidity of movement and was planned to be completed within 24 hours, during which time it was proposed to penetrate the 'Hindenburg Line'.

At the training centres Tanks were overhauled and fitted with a specially designed device to enable them to cross the three rows of the Hindenburg Line trenches, which were known to be some twelve feet wide (3.6M), eighteen feet (5.4M) deep, and the span of the Mark IV Tank was only ten feet (3.0M). This device consisted of binding together with chains some seventy five ordinary fascines of brushwood, strongly compressed. It was to be carried on the nose of the Tank and could be released from an internal position and dropped neatly into a trench. Central Tank Workshops manufactured 350 fascines in three weeks utilising 21,000 ordinary stout bundles of brushwood normally used for road repairing. On completion each completed fascine weighed a ton and a half; each Tank could only carry one fascine, and once it had been dropped into a trench, it could not be recovered again by that Tank without considerable difficulty.

The plan for the attack was divided into areas for three Tanks who formed a section and worked together. Of these one was an Advance Guard Tank and the other two Infantry Tanks. The

Advance Tanks duty was to travel forward through the enemy's wire, and turning to the left without crossing the trench in front of it, opening fire on the enemy from its right hand sponsons to protect the two advancing Infantry Tanks. These Tanks then travelled to the same position, the first dropping its fascine into the first trench, crossing over it and turning left firing from its right sponson. The second Infantry Tank followed suit, crossing the second trench, then followed by the Advance Tank casting its fascine and crossing the third trench.

The 'Hindenburg Line' was a defensive structure several kilometres in width from the North Sea to the town of Verdun in five heavily fortified operational sections, or *Stellungen,* which were named from north to south from figures of German mythology; Wotan, Siegfried, Alberich, Brunhild and Kriemhild. The trenches were organised in three parallel lines, separated out by a distance of some 600 to 800 metres (650 – 866 yards). Each trench-line was protected by a barbed wire entanglement, concrete bunkers and pill boxes; armaments consisted of machine guns, trench mortars and field guns.

The priority for the attack was the enemy's communication system; the vital railway network for both reinforcements and munitions in the area between the Escaut, the Sensee and the Canal du Nord and the Saint-Quentin Canal. The Canal du Nord had just been completed in 1917 and contained no water but formed an impassable barrier thirty metres (98 ft) deep. The terrain was well drained chalk down-land, which had not been disturbed by heavy shelling and provided perfect ground conditions on which the Tanks could operate.

Concealment of the nightly shifting of Tanks, infantry and artillery to their assembly areas, the isolation of the front from journalists, and a total security blackout all contributed to the radical originality of the plan of attack. The surprise was enhanced by ensuring that communication systems by wireless telegraphy and telephone were also strictly controlled to give an impression of normality behind the British lines.

Marcoing was to be the objective village for the two battalions 'A' and 'B' who advanced on both sides of the railway line along the valley of Couillet Wood. Cyril who was in No 11 Section, 3rd Company, 'A' Battalion under the command of Captain D T Raikes, was in a group of four Tanks with orders to cross the canal. The only possible route was by way of the main railway bridge which was constructed of high sided plate girders supporting a single rail-track. The high sides of the narrow bridge prevented 'male' Tanks passing over, whilst the more compact sponsons of the 'female' Tank made it possible for them to negotiate the bridge. Cyril was crewed to Tank A55, 'Aggressive II', Se2878, under the command of 2nd Lt J Lipscomb, which crossed the canal and cleared enemy machine guns firing from Talma Chateau and then travelled on towards the 87th Brigades final objective at Flots Farm. The other three Tanks - A52, A53 and A54 later returned to their rallying point at Marcoing railway station. A55 was lost and, although they did not know it, this Tank was the one that got closest of all the Tanks on that day to Cambrai.

At dusk, two of the crew of A55 arrived and reported the Tank was out of action and the remainder of the crew had been killed or injured. A55, Cyril's Tank, had received a direct hit from a shell wounding Lipscomb severely shattering his right arm with wounds to his right side and face. His NCO and two of his crew assisted him towards the British lines but, within 150 yards (138M) of them, he collapsed completely. The rest of the party then went on to obtain a stretcher on which to carry him, but the Germans had made a small advance and it was impossible to get near him, one of the crew being shot in the process, so ended Cyril's life. Lipscombe was captured and outlived the war as a prisoner. Crew members

Corporal A J Squire, Pte E Scholey were also killed in the shelled Tank.

During the following day on an attack on Rumilly at 12:30, it was discovered that 'Aggressive II' A55 was being utilised by the Germans as a machine gun nest firing on the Tanks of its old section. A German officer, Leutnant Quehl, Reserve Infanterie Regiment 227, 107th Division, claimed credit for the destruction of A55, claiming it was infantry with armour piercing ammunition and not the artillery which were responsible for knocking out the Tank. On the approach of darkness and examining the abandoned Tank they discovered good 'booty' within it, cake containing raisins, chocolate, cognac and champagne.

A letter from one of Cyril's fellow 'tankies' from the battlefield, Gunner H W Hensman, to Cyril's mother Sarah stated, "Dear Madam, It is with deep regret that I am writing to inform you of the death of your brave son. I am very sorry to say that he was killed on the morning of the 20th, we are all very sorry to lose such a good comrade, he was always the first to do anything for anyone of us, and if it will help you to bear your sorrow, I don't think he suffered any pain as it was instant death, and he was the same as he always has been, as brave and as good a soldier as ever served his King and Country. I for one shall always miss him as he was like a brother to me as we always shared what we had with each other, and he asked me to write to you if anything happened to him, also to send some things home for him, which I will do if ever I am spared to get back to camp again. I now conclude with deepest sorrow with you."

So, sadly, finished the gallant life of Gunner Cyril Sheldon Allen DCM on November 20th 1917, of 25 years and 12 days, his remains were never repatriated to a named grave, but his life is celebrated on The Louverval Memorial to the Missing, near Cambrai, France, he is also remembered on the Scunthorpe War Memorial, St Andrews Church Memorial Plaque- Burton upon Stather, John Lysaghts Steelworks Memorial now at North Lincolnshire Museum, Tank Memorial Ypres Salient-Poelcapelle-Flanders, and Burton upon Stather War Memorial.

Commemorative Plaque installed on the wall of the Merlijn Restaurant, Beselare, overlooking Polygon Wood.

During April 2015, a special memorial plaque to Captain Clement Robertson, VC, and Gunner Cyril Sheldon Allen, DCM, was dedicated in the grounds of the Merlijn Restaurant, Beselare. Also in the grounds, a flagstaff overlooking Polygon Wood, where the gallant action of these two brave men took place, saw the permanent raising of the Tank Corps Colours, brown, red and green, interpreted to symbolise 'from mud, through blood, to the green fields beyond'.

The motto of the Tank Corps is 'Fear Naught' and the ancient Allen family motto is 'Non Sibi', which interpreted into English from Latin, means 'Not for Himself', certainly a true phrase in Cyril Sheldon Allen's short life.

Chapter 8   The Distinguished Conduct Medal

The Distinguished Conduct Medal, post nominal letters DCM, which Cyril was awarded, is the oldest British award for gallantry, and was established by Queen Victoria and instituted by Royal Warrant on 4th December 1854, as a decoration for gallantry in the field by other ranks of the British Army.

Distinguished Conduct Medal
laid across the original box as sent to Cyril's father

For all ranks below commissioned officers, it was the second highest award for gallantry in action after the Victoria Cross and the other ranks equivalent of the Distinguished Service Order, which was awarded to commissioned officers for bravery.

The medal was struck in silver and is a disk, 1.4 inches (36mm) in diameter and 0.12 inches (3mm) thick. The ribbon suspender is an ornamental scroll pattern and the recipient's number, rank, forename initials, surname and unit are engraved on the rim.

The obverse of Cyril's medal shows the effigy of King George V, bareheaded, with the respective titles of the monarch inscribed around the perimeter 'GEORGIVS V BRITT: OMN: REX ET IND: IMP.'

The reverse is smooth with a raised rim and bears the inscription 'FOR DISTINGUISHED CONDUCT IN THE FIELD' underlined by a laurel wreath between two spear heads.

In a review of the British honours system in 1993, that formed part of the drive to remove distinctions of rank in respect of rewards for bravery, the DCM was discontinued along with the Conspicuous Gallantry Medal and the Distinguished Service Order. These decorations were replaced by the Conspicuous Gallantry Cross to serve as a second level reward to all ranks, of all British armed services.

Both Cyril's silver British War Medal 1914-1918, bronze/brass WW1 Victory Medal and DCM, are in good condition in my safe-keeping.

Chapter 9   Next of Kin Memorial Plaque and Scroll

All those who died whilst on military service in the battlegrounds of the Great War between 4th August 1914 and 30th April 1919, were commemmorated on a plaque and a scroll.

In October 1916, the British Government set up a committee selected from the House of Commons and the House of Lords and other departments, regarding the idea for a commemorative memorial plaque that could be given to relatives of deceased soldiers. In August 1917 a competition was open to all British born subjects for a suitable design.

The winner was Mr Carter-Preston, a painter and sculptor, who was awarded £250 for his design, the results being announced in The Times on 20th March 1918. The design incorporates the figure of Britannia, facing to her left and holding a laurel wreath in her left hand over a box which commemorates the deceased's name. In her right hand she is holding a trident with two sea dolphins on her left and right sides, with a growling lion at her feet.

The words "HE DIED FOR FREEDOM AND HONOUR" were written around the margin of the 4½ inch (11.43cm) bronze plaque, the letters E CR P near the lions right paw being the initials of the designer. Production did not start until December 1918 at the Governments War Memorial Plaque Factory, 54-56 Church Road, Acton, London W3.

From 1919 the British Army records offices sent out Army Form W.5080 to the next named of kin in a deceased soldiers Service Record. The next of kin had to complete details on the form for their relationship, ie: mother, father, widow, children etc, signing the declaration in their own handwriting and counter-signed by a Minister or Magistrate.

Next of kin Memorial Plaque

The memorial plaques were sent to the next of kin enclosed in a brown thick card folder, with an enclosed certificate headlined, 'Buckingham Palace' stating: I join with my grateful people in sending this memorial of a brave life given for others in the Great War. George. R.I.

BUCKINGHAM PALACE.

I join with my grateful people
in sending you this memorial
of a brave life given for others
in the Great War.

George R.I.

In October 1917, it was announced that the committee had also decided to issue a commemmorative scroll to the next of kin, printed on high quality paper size 11 x 7 inches (27 x 17cm). The text was printed in calligraphic script beneath the Royal Crest followed in script with the deceased's rank, name and regiment.

Both the scroll and plaque of Cyril Sheldon Allen remain in good condition in my safe-keep.

Gv RI

HE whom this scroll commemorates
was numbered among those who,
at the call of King and Country, left all
that was dear to them, endured hardness,
faced danger, and finally passed out of
the sight of men by the path of duty
and self-sacrifice, giving up their own
lives that others might live in freedom.

Let those who come after see to it
that his name be not forgotten.

Gunner Cyril Sheldon Allen, D.C.M.
Tank Corps

No. 200195. Pte. Cyril S. Allen.

Heavy Branch, Machine Gun Corps.

I have read with much Interest the
Report of your Commanding Officer
on your grit and determination
under heavy fire on the 1st and
3rd Oct. 1917. 3rd Battle of Ypres.
This reflects credit on yourself and
the good name of the Heavy Branch.

A certificate of commendation signed and sent by
Brigadier General Hugh Elles to Cyril after the 3rd Battle of Ypres.

The Cambrai Memorial commemorates more than 7,030 servicemen of the UK and South Africa who died in the Battle of Cambrai in 1917 and whose graves are not known. The Memorial stands on a terrace on the Louvervai Military Cemetery which is situated on the north side of the N30, Baupaume to Cambrai road. C S Allen DCM is remembered on Panel 13.

References

I acknowledge references made to the following publications during my research, in addition to family records and photographs, also material forwarded to me by Mr Peter Allen.

Major C William-Ellis MC. (1915), The Tank Corps

JFC Fuller (1920), Tanks in the Great War

R Baccarne, Poelcapelle 1917

J L Gibot, P Gorczynski, (1999), Following the Tanks, Cambrai

B Hammond, (2008), Cambrai 1917

D Dougan, (1970), The Great Gun-Maker

T Pidgeon, (2010), Tanks on the Somme

The War Histories and War Experiences of the 1st Tank Btn, Tank Corps

Various War Diaries

The Hull Times, (1913/17)

Archive material of the MGC Old Comrades Association

Archive material from the Tank Museum, Bovington